TUBA
101 HIT SONGS

Available for
FLUTE, CLARINET, ALTO SAX, TENOR SAX, TRUMPET,
HORN, TROMBONE, TUBA, VIOLIN, VIOLA, CELLO

ISBN 978-1-70514-709-2

Visit Hal Leonard Online at
www.halleonard.com

Contact us:
Hal Leonard
7777 West Bluemound Road
Milwaukee, WI 53213
Email: info@halleonard.com

In Europe, contact:
Hal Leonard Europe Limited
42 Wigmore Street
Marylebone, London, W1U 2RN
Email: info@halleonardeurope.com

In Australia, contact:
Hal Leonard Australia Pty. Ltd.
4 Lentara Court
Cheltenham, Victoria, 3192 Australia
Email: info@halleonard.com.au

CONTENTS

ALL ABOUT THAT BASS

Tuba

Words and Music by KEVIN KADISH
and MEGHAN TRAINOR

AMAZED

Tuba

Words and Music by MARV GREEN,
CHRIS LINDSEY and AIMEE MAYO

Moderately slow

ALL OF ME

Tuba

Words and Music by JOHN STEPHENS
and TOBY GAD

Slowly, in 2

APOLOGIZE

TUBA

Words and Music by
RYAN TEDDER

BEAUTIFUL

TUBA

Words and Music by
LINDA PERRY

Moderately slow

BAD DAY

TUBA

Words and Music by
DANIEL POWTER

Moderate groove

D.S. al Coda

CODA

BAD ROMANCE

Tuba

Words and Music by STEFANI GERMANOTTA
and NADIR KHAYAT

BEAUTIFUL DAY

TUBA

Words by BONO
Music by U2

Moderately

BEAUTIFUL IN MY EYES

Tuba

Words and Music by
JOSHUA KADISON

BECAUSE I LOVE YOU
(The Postman Song)

TUBA

Words and Music by
WARREN BROOKS

Slowly

BELIEVE

Tuba

Words and Music by BRIAN HIGGINS,
STUART McLENNEN, PAUL BARRY,
STEPHEN TORCH, MATT GRAY
and TIM POWELL

BUTTERFLY KISSES

TUBA

Words and Music by BOB CARLISLE
and RANDY THOMAS

BRAVE

Tuba

Words and Music by SARA BAREILLES
and JACK ANTONOFF

BREAKAWAY
from THE PRINCESS DIARIES 2: ROYAL ENGAGEMENT

Tuba

Words and Music by BRIDGET BENENATE,
AVRIL LAVIGNE and MATTHEW GERRARD

BREATHE

TUBA

Words and Music by HOLLY LAMAR
and STEPHANIE BENTLEY

Moderately fast

CALL ME MAYBE

Tuba

Words and Music by CARLY RAE JEPSEN,
JOSHUA RAMSAY and TAVISH CROWE

Moderately

To Coda ⊕

D.S. al Coda
(no repeat)

CODA
⊕

CANDLE IN THE WIND 1997

Tuba

Words and Music by ELTON JOHN
and BERNIE TAUPIN

Slowly, in 2

CHANGE THE WORLD

featured on the Motion Picture Soundtrack PHENOMENON

Tuba

Words and Music by WAYNE KIRKPATRICK,
GORDON KENNEDY and TOMMY SIMS

Moderately

CHASING CARS

Tuba

Words and Music by GARY LIGHTBODY,
TOM SIMPSON, PAUL WILSON,
JONATHAN QUINN and NATHAN CONNOLLY

THE CLIMB
from HANNAH MONTANA: THE MOVIE

TUBA

Words and Music by JESSI ALEXANDER
and JON MABE

Moderately slow

CLOCKS

Tuba

Words and Music by GUY BERRYMAN,
JON BUCKLAND, WILL CHAMPION
and CHRIS MARTIN

DON'T KNOW WHY

TUBA

Words and Music by
JESSE HARRIS

COUNTDOWN

Tuba

Words and Music by BEYONCÉ KNOWLES,
CAINON LAMB, JULIE FROST, MICHAEL BIVINS,
ESTHER DEAN, TERIUS NASH, SHEA TAYLOR,
NATHAN MORRIS and WANYA MORRIS

2nd time, D.C. al Coda

CODA

CRUISE

Tuba

Words and Music by CHASE RICE,
TYLER HUBBARD, BRIAN KELLEY,
JOEY MOI and JESSE RICE

Moderately, in 2

37

CRYIN'

Tuba

Words and Music by STEVEN TYLER,
JOE PERRY and TAYLOR RHODES

DIE A HAPPY MAN

Tuba

Words and Music by THOMAS RHETT,
JOE SPARGUR and SEAN DOUGLAS

Moderately slow

DILEMMA

Tuba

Words and Music by CORNELL HAYNES,
ANTWON MAKER, KENNETH GAMBLE
and BUNNY SIGLER

Moderately slow, in 2

Fine

2nd time, D.S. al Fine

44

DRIFT AWAY

Tuba

Words and Music by
MENTOR WILLIAMS

Moderately fast

FIELDS OF GOLD

TUBA

Music and Lyrics by
STING

DROPS OF JUPITER
(Tell Me)

Tuba

Words and Music by PAT MONAHAN,
JAMES STAFFORD, ROBERT HOTCHKISS,
CHARLES COLIN and SCOTT UNDERWOOD

D.S. al Coda

CODA

FALLIN'

Tuba

Words and Music by
ALICIA KEYS

FIREWORK

Tuba

Words and Music by KATY PERRY,
MIKKEL ERIKSEN, TOR ERIK HERMANSEN,
ESTHER DEAN and SANDY WILHELM

Moderately

FOOLISH GAMES

TUBA

Words and Music by
JEWEL KILCHER

Slowly

FOREVER AND FOR ALWAYS

Tuba

Words and Music by SHANIA TWAIN
and R.J. LANGE

Moderately, in 2

FRIENDS IN LOW PLACES

Tuba

Words and Music by DeWAYNE BLACKWELL
and EARL BUD LEE

FROM A DISTANCE

TUBA

Words and Music by
JULIE GOLD

Moderately slow

GENIE IN A BOTTLE

Tuba

Words and Music by STEVE KIPNER,
DAVID FRANK and PAMELA SHEYNE

GET LUCKY

Tuba

Words and Music by THOMAS BANGALTER,
GUY MANUEL HOMEM CHRISTO, NILE RODGERS
and PHARRELL WILLIAMS

Moderately

HOW TO SAVE A LIFE

Tuba

Words and Music by JOSEPH KING
and ISAAC SLADE

Moderately fast

HELLO

Tuba

Words and Music by ADELE ADKINS
and GREG KURSTIN

HERE AND NOW

Tuba

Words and Music by TERRY STEELE
and DAVID ELLIOT

Moderately slow

HERO

Tuba

Words and Music by ENRIQUE IGLESIAS,
PAUL BARRY and MARK TAYLOR

Moderately slow

HEY, SOUL SISTER

Tuba

Words and Music by PAT MONAHAN,
ESPEN LIND and AMUND BJORKLUND

HO HEY

Tuba

Words and Music by JEREMY FRAITES
and WESLEY SCHULTZ

Moderately slow, in 2

HOLD ON, WE'RE GOING HOME

Tuba

Words and Music by AUBREY GRAHAM,
PAUL JEFFERIES, NOAH SHEBIB,
JORDAN ULLMAN and MAJID AL-MASKATI

Moderately

HOME

Tuba

Words and Music by GREG HOLDEN
and DREW PEARSON

Moderately, in 2

THE HOUSE THAT BUILT ME

Tuba

Words and Music by TOM DOUGLAS
and ALLEN SHAMBLIN

Moderately, in 2

77

HOW AM I SUPPOSED TO LIVE WITHOUT YOU

Tuba

Words and Music by MICHAEL BOLTON
and DOUG JAMES

Slowly, in 2

I FINALLY FOUND SOMEONE

from THE MIRROR HAS TWO FACES

Tuba

Words and Music by BARBRA STREISAND,
MARVIN HAMLISCH, R.J. LANGE
and BRYAN ADAMS

Moderately slow

I GOTTA FEELING

Tuba

Words and Music by WILL ADAMS,
ALLAN PINEDA, JAIME GOMEZ, STACY FERGUSON,
DAVID GUETTA and FREDERIC RIESTERER

Moderately fast

I KISSED A GIRL

Tuba

Words and Music by KATY PERRY,
CATHY DENNIS, MAX MARTIN
and LUKASZ GOTTWALD

Moderately

I SWEAR

TUBA

Words and Music by FRANK MYERS
and GARY BAKER

I WILL REMEMBER YOU

Theme from THE BROTHERS McMULLEN

Tuba

Words and Music by SARAH McLACHLAN,
SEAMUS EGAN and DAVE MERENDA

Moderately slow

JAR OF HEARTS

TUBA

Words and Music by BARRETT YERETSIAN,
CHRISTINA PERRI and DREW LAWRENCE

Moderately slow

JUST THE WAY YOU ARE

TUBA

Words and Music by BRUNO MARS,
ARI LEVINE, PHILIP LAWRENCE,
KHARI CAIN and KHALIL WALTON

LIPS OF AN ANGEL

Tuba

Words and Music by AUSTIN WINKLER,
ROSS HANSON, LLOYD GARVEY, MARK KING,
MICHAEL RODDEN and BRIAN HOWES

Slowly

LITTLE TALKS

Tuba

Words and Music by
OF MONSTERS AND MEN

LET IT GO

TUBA

Words and Music by JAMES BAY
and PAUL BARRY

NEED YOU NOW

Tuba

Words and Music by HILLARY SCOTT,
CHARLES KELLEY, DAVE HAYWOOD
and JOSH KEAR

LOSING MY RELIGION

Tuba

Words and Music by WILLIAM BERRY,
PETER BUCK, MICHAEL MILLS
and MICHAEL STIPE

Moderately fast

LOVE SONG

Tuba

Words and Music by
SARA BAREILLES

LOVE STORY

TUBA

Words and Music by
TAYLOR SWIFT

Moderately

MORE THAN WORDS

Tuba

Words and Music by NUNO BETTENCOURT
and GARY CHERONE

Moderately slow

NO ONE

Tuba

Words and Music by ALICIA KEYS,
KERRY BROTHERS, JR. and GEORGE HARRY

Moderately

100 YEARS

TUBA

Words and Music by
JOHN ONDRASIK

REHAB

TUBA

Words and Music by
AMY WINEHOUSE

THE POWER OF LOVE

Tuba

Words by MARY SUSAN APPLEGATE
and JENNIFER RUSH
Music by CANDY DEROUGE
and GUNTHER MENDE

Slowly

ROAR

Tuba

Words and Music by KATY PERRY,
MAX MARTIN, DR. LUKE,
BONNIE McKEE and HENRY WALTER

ROLLING IN THE DEEP

Tuba

Words and Music by ADELE ADKINS
and PAUL EPWORTH

ROYALS

Tuba

Words and Music by ELLA YELICH-O'CONNOR
and JOEL LITTLE

Moderately

Save the Best for Last

Tuba

Words and Music by WENDY WALDMAN,
PHIL GALDSTON and JON LIND

SAY SOMETHING

Tuba

Words and Music by IAN AXEL,
CHAD VACCARINO and MIKE CAMPBELL

Very slowly, in 4

SHAKE IT OFF

Tuba

Words and Music by TAYLOR SWIFT,
MAX MARTIN and SHELLBACK

SECRETS

TUBA

Words and Music by
RYAN TEDDER

Moderately slow, in 2

SHE WILL BE LOVED

TUBA

Words and Music by ADAM LEVINE
and JAMES VALENTINE

SMELLS LIKE TEEN SPIRIT

TUBA

Words and Music by KURT COBAIN,
KRIST NOVOSELIC and DAVE GROHL

SOMETHING TO TALK ABOUT
(Let's Give Them Something to Talk About)

TUBA

Words and Music by
SHIRLEY EIKHARD

STAY WITH ME

Tuba

Words and Music by SAM SMITH,
JAMES NAPIER, WILLIAM EDWARD PHILLIPS,
TOM PETTY and JEFF LYNNE

STACY'S MOM

Tuba

Words and Music by CHRIS COLLINGWOOD
and ADAM SCHLESINGER

Medium Rock

STAY

TUBA

Words and Music by MIKKY EKKO
and JUSTIN PARKER

Moderately

STRONGER
(What Doesn't Kill You)

Tuba

Words and Music by GREG KURSTIN,
JORGEN ELOFSSON, DAVID GAMSON
and ALEXANDRA TAMPOSI

Moderately

2nd time, to Coda
3rd time, Fine

D.S. al Coda

CODA

D.S. al Fine

TEARS IN HEAVEN

Tuba

Words and Music by ERIC CLAPTON
and WILL JENNINGS

TEENAGE DREAM

Tuba

Words and Music by KATY PERRY,
BONNIE McKEE, LUKASZ GOTTWALD,
MAX MARTIN and BENJAMIN LEVIN

THINKING OUT LOUD

Tuba

Words and Music by ED SHEERAN
and AMY WADGE

Moderately slow

THIS LOVE

TUBA

Words and Music by ADAM LEVINE
and JESSE CARMICHAEL

Moderate Rock

A THOUSAND YEARS

from the Summit Entertainment film THE TWILIGHT SAGE: BREAKING DAWN - PART 1

Tuba

Words and Music by DAVID HODGES
and CHRISTINA PERRI

Slowly, in 1

TILL THE WORLD ENDS

Tuba

Words and Music by LUKASZ GOTTWALD,
MAX MARTIN, KESHA SEBERT
and ALEXANDER KRONLUND

Moderately fast

UPTOWN FUNK

Words and Music by MARK RONSON,
BRUNO MARS, PHILIP LAWRENCE, JEFF BHASKER, DEVON GALLASPY,
NICHOLAUS WILLIAMS, LONNIE SIMMONS, RONNIE WILSON,
CHARLES WILSON, RUDOLPH TAYLOR and ROBERT WILSON

VIVA LA VIDA

Tuba

Words and Music by GUY BERRYMAN,
JON BUCKLAND, WILL CHAMPION
and CHRIS MARTIN

Moderately

WAITING ON THE WORLD TO CHANGE

TUBA

Words and Music by
JOHN MAYER

WE CAN'T STOP

Tuba

Words and Music by MILEY CYRUS,
THERON THOMAS, TIMOTHY THOMAS, MICHAEL WILLIAMS,
PIERRE SLAUGHTER, DOUGLAS DAVIS and RICKY WALTERS

Moderately slow

WE BELONG TOGETHER

Tuba

Words and Music by MARIAH CAREY,
JERMAINE DUPRI, MANUEL SEAL, JOHNTA AUSTIN,
DARNELL BRISTOL, KENNETH EDMONDS, SIDNEY JOHNSON,
PATRICK MOTEN, BOBBY WOMACK and SANDRA SULLY

WE FOUND LOVE

TUBA

Words and Music by
CALVIN HARRIS

WHAT MAKES YOU BEAUTIFUL

TUBA

Words and Music by SAVAN KOTECHA,
RAMI YACOUB and CARL FALK

WHEN YOU SAY NOTHING AT ALL

Tuba

Words and Music by DON SCHLITZ
and PAUL OVERSTREET

YOU RAISE ME UP

Tuba

Words and Music by BRENDAN GRAHAM
and ROLF LOVLAND

Moderately slow

small notes optional

YEAH!

Tuba

Words and Music by JAMES PHILLIPS,
LA MARQUIS JEFFERSON, CHRISTOPHER BRIDGES,
JONATHAN SMITH and SEAN GARRETT

YOU WERE MEANT FOR ME

Tuba

Words and Music by JEWEL MURRAY
and STEVE POLTZ

To Coda

Slowly, freely

D.C. al Coda

CODA

YOU'RE BEAUTIFUL

Tuba

Words and Music by JAMES BLUNT,
SACHA SKARBEK and AMANDA GHOST

YOU'RE STILL THE ONE

Tuba

Words and Music by SHANIA TWAIN
and R.J. LANGE

YOU'VE GOT A FRIEND IN ME

from Walt Disney's TOY STORY

TUBA

Music and Lyrics by
RANDY NEWMAN